# Your Church Wants to Hear from You

*What Is the Synod on Synodality?*

Michael J. Sanem

**LITURGICAL PRESS**

Collegeville, Minnesota

www.litpress.org

Cover design by Monica Bokinskie.
Art courtesy of Getty Images.

ISBN 978-0-8146-6816-0    978-0-8146-6817-7 (e-book)

© 2022 by Michael J. Sanem

Published by Liturgical Press, Collegeville, Minnesota. All rights reserved. No part of this book may be used or reproduced in any manner whatsoever, except brief quotations in reviews, without written permission of Liturgical Press, Saint John's Abbey, PO Box 7500, Collegeville, MN 56321-7500. Printed in the United States of America.

*For Megan, who holds it all together,
and William, George, and Nicholas,
who teach us about love.*

# Introduction
# Your Church Wants to Hear from You

In October 2021, the Catholic Church officially began the largest consultative process in human history. The entire people of God, some 1.34 billion Catholics worldwide, were asked to participate in a process of listening and engagement together over the course of two years. Why embark on this incredibly novel, time-consuming, and expensive task? Because your church wants to hear from you.

Pope Francis, in union with the bishops of the church, have discerned that "it is precisely this path of synodality which God expects of the Church of the third millennium."[1] While in the past a synod was

---

1. Synod of Bishops, *For a Synodal Church: Communion, Participation, and Mission*, Preparatory Document for the Synod 2021–2023 (hereafter, Preparatory Document), para. 1, quoting

reserved only for bishops, this "Synod on Synodality" consults the entire people of God: lay and ordained, religious and nonreligious, Catholic and beyond. This marks a new and more expansive understanding of synodality. It is a recovery of a way of being church that is deeply embedded in our ecclesiology, theology, and history. God, through the workings of the Holy Spirit, is doing something new in this moment. We are responding by recovering an ancient and fruitful way of being church together: the synodal way.

Think of all the changes in culture and society that have happened in the past few decades, years, or even months! We've experienced a global pandemic, widespread political and social upheaval, and deep divisions in our church, culture, and society. Even families and friends are struggling with polarization and division. The church continues to grapple with the sex abuse crisis, and the cultural history of clericalism has made it difficult to institute greater transparency and accountability. In many parts of the world, Christians are being violently persecuted. There are deeply divisive debates about the role of religion in society and political life.[2]

---

Pope Francis's address for the Ceremony Commemorating the 50th Anniversary of the Institution of the Synod of Bishops (17 October 2015), https://www.synod.va/en/documents/english-version-of-the-preparatory-document.html.

2. Preparatory Document, para. 4–8.

Responding to these challenges requires listening, dialogue, and discernment. All people are necessary and play an important role. This is synodality. In short, this isn't just another meeting or list of to-dos. Instead, it is the beginning of a "conversion process" that is essential to the life of the church and its mission. And the church needs *you* to carry it out.

This short booklet sketches out the main objectives and process of the 2021–2023 synod, including the ten themes (or nuclei of synodality) that the synod explores. It also highlights the historical and theological roots of this new approach to synodality. I hope that this will inspire you to get involved with the local phase of the synod to build a church that listens, heals, and dialogues. In doing so we may all "journey together" with Christ into a hope-filled future.

# The Goal of the Synod on Synodality

The key to understanding the Synod on Synodality can be better illuminated by the popular phrase: "the journey is the destination." The goal is to become a church that "journeys together." How does this journeying on both local and universal levels allow the church to proclaim the Gospel? How does the Spirit invite us to grow as a synodal church? To fully answer these questions, we need the entire church to listen and learn from each other and the Holy Spirit.

Because the "the journey is the destination," the Synod on Synodality represents an opening movement in a much larger process. This pilot experience makes it possible to grow in synodality through synodality. By engaging in this process we hope to become a church that fosters dialogue and listening among all people, especially the poor and vulnerable. This process makes room for all the people of God to be heard and exercise leadership in accord with the common priesthood of all the baptized.

The Preparatory Document for the Synod presents ten "nuclei" or themes for each local church to reflect upon. Consider how you might respond given your unique cultural and local situation, and the presence of the Holy Spirit moving in your life:

1. Companions on the Journey: Who do we consider a part of "our church"? Who is left out? Who "journeys together"? Who is left behind?

2. A Listening Church: As a church, to whom do we listen? Do we listen with open minds and hearts? How do we listen to laypeople, particularly women and young people? Do we create space for minorities and those who are discarded and excluded by society? What prejudices and stereotypes hinder our listening? Do we listen for the unique realities of the society and culture in which we live?

3. Speaking Out: How do we promote free and authentic communication within our community? How do we invite everyone to speak with courage, truth, and charity? How do we communicate with the wider communities and society? How do we communicate with the media,

including Catholic media? Who speaks as a representative for the Christian community?

4. Celebrating: How is our "journeying together" connected to our celebration of Eucharist? How do prayer and liturgy "inspire and direct" our journeying together? How do prayer and liturgy inspire our discernment and decision-making? How can we promote full and active participation in our liturgical prayer?

5. Shared Responsibility for Mission: Do all the baptized feel a shared sense of mission? How does the church community support those who work for social justice, those who pursue scientific research, those who teach, those who protect human rights, and those who protect the environment? How do we collaborate in mission with other churches, Christian communities, religions, and social groups?

6. Dialogue in Church and Society: How do we dialogue together, both within the church and within the larger society? How do we address differences of opinion, vision, and experience? How do we collaborate with neighboring dioceses, religious communities, and lay associations and movements? How do we dialogue with members of other religions? How do we dialogue with the poor and marginalized? How

do we dialogue with others regarding politics, economics, and culture?

7. Dialogue with Other Christians: Do we feel united in one baptism with other Christians? What are the concerns and challenges within other Christian communities? What are the fruits of "journeying together" with other Christians?

8. Authority and Participation: How is authority exercised? Who exercises this authority? How are common goals identified and pursued? How are the voices of the laity upheld? How do we foster synodal-style conversation at the diocesan and parish level?

9. Discerning and Deciding: Do we make decisions in a synodal way—that is, through discernment, listening to one another and the Spirit, and gathering consensus? What are the procedures and methods we use to discern together? How can these procedures and methods be improved? How can we promote participation in decision-making within "hierarchically structured communities"? How can we promote greater transparency and accountability within the church?

10. Forming Ourselves in Synodality: How do we form people and communities to "journey to-

gether"? How do we form those who hold responsibility within the church to listen and engage in dialogue? How do we understand our own cultural context? How does our particular culture affect our understanding of church?[1]

These are the main themes explored during the first phase of the synod, which began in October 2021 and ends in August 2022. This first phase is where local churches and dioceses listen to people in their local communities. Once the results of these sessions are compiled, they are sent to regional groups of bishops (such as the United States Conference of Catholic Bishops), where they are further synthesized and summarized before being sent to the Vatican. Regional and continental pre-synodal meetings will take place, with the final documents produced by March 2023. In October of 2023, the Synod of Bishops will convene in Rome and bring together representatives from around the world to listen, discern, and reflect on how we can become a more synodal church. A synodal church encourages the participation of all the people of God, especially the marginalized, in the mission of the church to accompany and evangelize the world.

---

1. Preparatory Document, para. 30.

# The Roots of a New Synodality

Many of us grew up with a fixed view of how the church should be organized and little awareness of the deep scriptural, theological, historical, and spiritual roots of synodality. To remind us of this, the Preparatory Document for the Synod outlines how synodality is essential to our mission and an integral element of our life together as church. The Preparatory Document also recalls the many gospel accounts where a diverse group of people, including the apostles, works together with Jesus. We can think of these accounts as an early example of a synodal experience, because each one of these players—Jesus, the crowd, and the apostles—must be present for a synodal church to exist. If Jesus is absent, then the crowd and the apostles fight for power and authority. If the crowd is absent, the apostles become isolated in their own understanding of religion and evangelization. If the apostles are absent, then the link to Jesus and the Spirit given by Christ to the apostles is broken, and Jesus is reduced to "myth" or "ideology."[1]

Drawing upon these gospel accounts, we see that our understanding of God, the church, and the sacraments are steeped in synodality. The church is grounded in communion. Our baptism and confirmation empower us, as we share the common dignity and mission of the church to evangelize and consecrate the world to God. As St. Paul describes, we are all the mystical Body of Christ in the world, blessed with a variety of gifts and charisms. Although our church is hierarchical in structure with particular teaching authority given to the magisterium, "God furnishes the totality of the faithful with an instinct of faith—*sensus fidei*—which helps them to discern what is truly of God."[2]

In *Lumen Gentium,* the Dogmatic Constitution on the Church, we see the expansive ecclesial and synodal vision set forth by the Second Vatican Council. *Lumen Gentium* names the mystery of the church, the people of God, and finally the hierarchical structure of the church.[3] Pope Francis describes this way of under-

---

1. Preparatory Document, para. 20.

2. International Theological Commission, *Synodality in the Life and Mission of the Church* (2 March 2018), para. 56, https://www.vatican.va/roman_curia/congregations/cfaith/cti_documents/rc_cti_20180302_sinodalita_en.html.

3. *Lumen Gentium* (Dogmatic Constitution on the Church), in Austin Flannery, ed., *Vatican Council II: Constitutions, De-*

standing church as an "inverted pyramid."[4] The communion of the entire people of God is at the top with *sensus fidei* guiding discernment. Below the people of God, the college of bishops recalls the teaching authority of the apostles. Finally, the pope, the successor of the apostle Peter, serves as the "rock" at the bottom, ensuring unity. The top of the pyramid is below the base, with those exercising authority becoming "ministers" in the truest sense of the word: "the least of all."[5]

We see this sense of synodality and *sensus fidei* active throughout our history, particularly in the first millennia of Christianity. A synodal style marked both the process and decision-making of the Apostolic Council of Jerusalem in AD 44 and the great Ecumenical Councils of Nicaea, Constantinople, Ephesus, and Chalcedon. All of these are essential to the foundations of Christianity. Though this synodal style weakened in the second millennia, with different developments in both the Roman Catholic Church and Eastern Orthodox Church, councils and synods continued. Over the past thousand years, however, a certain hierarchical style took root in the Roman Catholic

---

*crees, Declarations; The Basic Sixteen Documents* (Collegeville, MN: Liturgical Press, 2014).

4. Ceremony Commemorating the 50th Anniversary of the Institution of the Synod of Bishops.

5. International Theological Commission, *Synodality*, para. 54–57.

Church. Rather than consulting the laity directly, the pope and bishops acted in what they believed to be the sense of the faithful.[6]

The Second Vatican Council marked a return to the synodal roots of the church, and as the *Vademecum*, or Handbook for initiating the synod, makes clear:

> The Second Vatican Council reinvigorated the sense that all the baptised, both the hierarchy and the laity, are called to be active participants in the saving mission of the Church (LG, 32–33). The faithful have received the Holy Spirit in baptism and confirmation and are endowed with diverse gifts and charisms for the renewal and building up of the Church, as members of the Body of Christ. Thus the teaching authority of the Pope and the bishops is in dialogue with the *sensus fidelium*, the living voice of the People of God.[7]

Synodality is not opposed to the hierarchical function of the church. Rather, as Pope Francis remarks, "Synodality . . . offers us the most appropriate interpre-

---

6. International Theological Commission, para. 54–57.

7. Synod of Bishops, Vademecum *for the Synod on Synodality*, Official Handbook for Listening and Discernment in Local Churches (September 2021), para. 1.3, https://www.synod.va/content/dam/synod/document/common/vademecum/Vademecum-EN-A4.pdf.

tive framework for understanding the hierarchical ministry itself."[8] The image of the "inverted pyramid" with the "top at the base" comes to mind.

Synodality, therefore, is the great complement to the vision of church recovered in the Second Vatican Council, emphasizing that "all the faithful enjoy a true equality with regard to the dignity and the activity which they share in the building up of the body of Christ."[9] This way of understanding church emphasizes the need for all the baptized to participate in the salvific mission of evangelization in the world.

Pope Francis has shown a special interest in synods with topics ranging from family vocation and mission to ecclesial renewal grounded in the Second Vatican Council. The 2018 Synod on Young People and the 2019 Synod on the Amazon have further reinvigorated the movement toward a more consultative process in church governance. The 2021–2023 Synod on Synodality seeks to build upon the momentum of these widespread consultative processes to build an ever more synodal church.

---

8. Ceremony Commemorating the 50th Anniversary of the Institution of the Synod of Bishops.

9. *Lumen Gentium*, para. 32.

# Conclusion
# What Does This Mean for You?

By virtue of our baptism and confirmation, the Holy Spirit is living and active in our individual and shared lives. A new synodal awakening in our church enables all of us to share our unique gifts, talents, and insights with the greater church, both during this Synod on Synodality and beyond.

Following the local phase of the synod, diocesan teams in the United States will compile a ten-page synthesis to present to the United States Catholic Conference of Bishops in June 2022. These will be further synthesized by the USCCB and submitted to the Synod of Bishops in August 2022.

If the local phase of the synod is still active, you can contact your parish or diocese to see what opportunities are available to contribute. However, if that deadline has passed or you were unable to participate, you may submit a synthesis of your reflections, either as an individual or community, directly to the General Secretariat of the Synod by August 2022. You can download resources for the synod, including the Preparatory Document and Handbook for the local phase, at the synod website: https://www.synod.va/en.html. The synod website also contains contact information for the General Secretariat.

The Synod on Synodality initiates a process where church governance is more reflective of the common dignity of all the baptized. While the short-term goal is the creation of a "pilot experience" for this listening and sharing, the long-term goal is the creation of a more "Constitutively Synodal Church."[1] May the Synod on Synodality encourage all of us to reflect on how our local Catholic community is already synodal, as well as the ways we might grow in cooperation, listening, and inclusion. Additionally, may this Spirit-filled process inspire all of us to participate more fully and consciously in our local Catholic parishes as we "journey together" with Christ toward greater participation, communion, and a shared sense of mission.

---

1. Preparatory Document, sec. II.

# Bibliography

International Theological Commission. *Sensus Fidei in the Life of the Church* (2014). https://www.vatican.va/roman_curia/congregations/cfaith/cti_documents/rc_cti_20140610_sensus-fidei_en.html.

International Theological Commission. *Synodality in the Life and Mission of the Church* (2 March 2018). https://www.vatican.va/roman_curia/congregations/cfaith/cti_documents/rc_cti_20180302_sinodalita_en.html.

*Lumen Gentium* (Dogmatic Constitution on the Church). In Austin Flannery, ed., *Vatican Council II: Constitutions, Decrees, Declarations; The Basic Sixteen Documents*. Collegeville, MN: Liturgical Press, 2014.

Synod of Bishops. *For a Synodal Church: Communion, Participation, and Mission*, Preparatory Document for the Synod 2021–2023. https://www.synod.va/en/documents/english-version-of-the-preparatory-document.html.

Synod of Bishops. Vademecum *for the Synod on Synodality*, Official Handbook for Listening and Discernment in Local Churches (September 2021). https://www.synod.va/content/dam/synod/document/common/vademecum/Vademecum-EN-A4.pdf.

## *A Synodal Prayer*

Good and Gracious God
you are Father, Son, and Spirit,
a communion of love that overflows into
    all creation.
Help your church become ever more like you
united in love, one in the Spirit,
overflowing into and engaging with a
    suffering world.
Help us encounter one another
and those on the margins and peripheries
as we would encounter you.
Help us to love one another,
listen to one another,
learn from one another,
and discern how your Spirit
is speaking to the entire people of God.
As we journey together into deeper synodality,
that is, deeper love, deeper communion,
    deeper humility,
we ask all this in the name of Jesus the Christ
who holds all things together in love.
Amen.